TRUE LOVE RELATIONSHIP:

SECURE YOUR FUTURE WITH YOUR SOULMATE

BY

THEOPHILUS ROGERS

B.Eng

TABLE OF CONTENT

INTRODUCTION

A few signals can be named, love. Then again, a few different feelings and sentiments can be mistaken for adoration, however individuals before long understand that they are not genuine romance. Here is to seeing more about adoration and the inclination

What is love precisely?

If you have any desire to characterize love in one sentence, love is quite possibly of the most significant feeling people insight. It is a blend of fascination and closeness. The individual we feel drawn to or near is the individual we are, generally, infatuated with.

Such an individual can be a companion, parent, kin, or even our pet. Such love depends on a sensation of fascination or friendship

Love can be characterized in various ways since there are various sorts of affection. The response to the inquiry,

"What is love for you?" can vary for everybody, contingent upon the relationship in setting.

According to the Cambridge word reference, love is characterized as enjoying another grown-up without a doubt and being sincerely and physically drawn to them or having unmistakable inclinations of preferring a companion or individual in your loved ones.

While this is a more strict meaning of the word, love can be characterized in numerous alternate ways.

How to portray love?

Sensations of affection can be characterized as a mixture of different feelings. Love is mindful, sympathy, persistence, not being desirous, not having assumptions, allowing yourself and others an opportunity, and not hurrying. What is love, then? You inquire. Love has most frequently been utilized as a thing, however by and by, affection is an action word. It is about how we help others and the numerous ways we cause others to feel adored and really focused on.

CHAPTER 1

Many individuals might consider what is going on with adoration in a relationship. The response lies in the components of affection.

1. Care

Care is one of the essential components of affection.

Assuming that we love somebody, we care about them, their sentiments, and their prosperity. We might make a special effort to ensure they are OK, and even split the difference and penance our requirements and needs to give them what they need.

Related Reading: Simple Steps to Take Care of Your Relationships

2. Profound respect

Profound respect is extremely vital in adoration and connections.

Esteem can be for their rawness or in any event, for their psyche and character. Preferring somebody for their outer and interior self and regarding their contemplations is a fundamental component of affection.

3. Want

Want is both sexual and physical and mental.

Simply needing to invest more energy with somebody, being around them, and needing them - are portions of the craving you feel when you are infatuated with somebody

10 Things You Need To Know About True Love

Genuine affection is mysterious. Genuine affection is mystical–Right? All things considered, sort of. Yet, it's beyond what that, as anybody in a relationship can tell you. Peruse on to find ten things you really want to be aware of genuine romance.

1. Genuine affection isn't tied in with thinking of yourself as In another.

Try not to experience passionate feelings for, or believe you're enamored, in light of the fact that you need to track down yourself. Your personality isn't to be somebody's other half–it's to act naturally! Try not to get so cleared up in your accomplice that you become them. You needn't bother with to love their #1 band or read every one of the books they read. Keep your inclinations and leisure activities and you'll be more fascinating in, and keen on, your accomplice.

2. Self esteem is the most ideal way to track down genuine romance.

It seems like a banality, something your mother and lady friends let you know each time you were crying over a messed up heart, however its true you should cherish yourself before you can cherish any other person. Be OK with yourself, in any event, while you're having a terrible day. Know what your identity is, where it counts inside, and understand how you need to manage your life. Being enamored with yourself and having your life on target isn't just extraordinarily self-fulfilling, but at the same time they're truly alluring characteristics to an accomplice.

3. Genuine affection isn't requesting.

Your accomplice ought to never request that you change assuming you're really adored. What's more, in the event that you really love your accomplice, you shouldn't anticipate that he should change. You got into a relationship since you enjoyed one another, and you developed to cherish each other as you are. How could you have to transform somebody you love so profoundly? Acknowledge them as they are, and you'll receive that thought in kind.

4. Genuine affection permits you to act naturally.

Acting naturally before your accomplice can appear to be unnerving right away. Awakening with next to no cosmetics on, and your hair a wreck? Shouldn't something be said about him seeing you when you're sick–runny nose, red eyes what not? It's something you need to stay away from as long as you can. In any case, you shouldn't have that impression. At the point when you're infatuated, even the most terrible disease is a lovely encounter since it's worth the effort. Your accomplice assisting you through a muddled episode or kissing you with morning breath is a significant stage towards your future, and it shows the amount he really cherishes you.

5. Genuine affection works out easily.

Do you feel a little uncertain about your accomplice? Is it true or not that you don't know they're ideal for you? Assuming you're posing yourself an excessive number of inquiries about your accomplice, your relationship, and your future together, then you're most likely not in affection. At the point when you're genuinely enamored, you question nothing. It feels normal to accompany your accomplice, and you realize you can manage anything to accomplish that future you're longing for.

6. To get love, you should give love.

You can't be in a caring relationship on the off chance that you keep down. You can't involve love as a negotiating concession. Try not to tell your accomplice you love him just when he accomplishes something great around the house. Try not to treat him with utter disdain in the event that he commits an error. You need to cherish him constantly, no matter what his words or activities, since genuine affection is unrestricted. Assuming you give your accomplice this much love, you'll get it–and more!–in return.

7. Genuine affection depends on companionship.

So many TV show connections depend on companions who become hopelessly enamored over the long haul. It's an extraordinary reason, and a decent fantasy, however life isn't TV. You needn't bother with to be dearest companions with your accomplice since kindergarten for affection to endure. Yet, you should be companions with your accomplice. You should have the option to talk, share jokes, and appreciate every others' conversation. Over the long run, the actual enthusiasm might blur, yet evident fellowship will endure forever.

8. Genuine romance endures.

Recollect those relaxed connections where your better half cleaning his nose on your shower towel was sufficient to end it. Those connections are juvenile, and anything that you assumed you encountered wasn't love. At the point when you're really enamored, issues like this are simply little obstacles. No issue appears to be outlandish. You're eager to deal with anything, just to remain together.

9. Genuine romance is committed.

It's human instinct to be drawn to others, to permit your head to be turned by an alluring bystander. Try not to let this cause you to feel regretful. However long you're focused on your accomplice, your relationship is fine. At the point when you're really infatuated, you would rather not be with any other person. You can't envision investing your energy without your darling.

10. YOU are your first love.

Remember that you want to adore yourself. Confidence is significant, however it's not something you ought to accomplish and afterward discard once you're with your accomplice. You should remain in affection with yourself for as long as you can remember. Assuming you begin to loathe yourself or what you're doing, you really want to change barely to the point of remaining focused, remain consistent with yourself, and remain in affection with yourself.

CHAPTER 2

Perfect partner

The encapsulation of affection and organization. In our quick moving tumultuous world, which brags various types various individuals, we end up skimming through additional connections than we might want to find that one individual who can really open our locks.

Not simply anybody can satisfy you the way your perfect partner can. There's a universe of a distinction between your perfect partner, your heart's other half, and a daily existence accomplice an individual who comes up short on components to shape impeccably to you. Your perfect partner causes you to feel good, mended, and flawless, similar to no piece is absent from the riddle. A soul mate, then again, can be an extraordinary ally and long-term friend however is restricted in their ability to enhance your soul.

Components of a Soulmate

Your perfect partner causes you to feel good, mended, and flawless, similar to no piece is absent from the riddle. A soulmate, then again, can be an extraordinary ally and long-lasting sidekick however is restricted in their ability to enhance your soul.

A perfect partner is somebody who has locks that fit our endlessly keys to accommodate our locks. At the point when we have a good sense of security enough to open the locks, our most genuine selves step out and we can be totally and truly what our identity is." Ok, perfect partners. The encapsulation of affection and organization. In our quick moving tumultuous world, which brags various types various individuals, we end up skimming through additional connections than we might want to find that one individual who can really open our locks.

Not simply anybody can satisfy you the way your perfect partner can. There's a universe of a distinction between your perfect partner, your heart's other half, and a day to day existence accomplice an individual who misses the mark on components to shape impeccably to you. Your perfect partner causes you to feel good, mended, and unblemished, similar to no piece is absent from the riddle. A soul mate, then again, can be an extraordinary ally and long-lasting buddy yet is restricted in their ability to enhance your soul.

The majority of us stay in life-accomplice connections since we "settle," for a large number of reasons. We, first and foremost, may have a genuine inner mind dread of being distant from everyone else. Also, since we're organically intended to experience passionate feelings for, it's just normal that we match up in this world. In any case, we some of the time drag out what are intended to be brief connections and erroneously sink into them for good. A few connections should keep going for a specific period to finish off a karmic section of life, connections in which we're intended to have kids with our accomplice however not be guaranteed to stay with them, and connections that are outright confounding in light of the fact that a mixture of feelings doesn't permit us to see our fated way.

I've considered everything in my training to be a therapist, from couples who wedded their young life loves to individuals in their retirement years that actually battle with responsibility issues. The majority of us fall somewhere close to these two limits, implying that we encountered a few connections prior to viewing the individual we accept as our ideal pair. Whether you're as of now hitched, in a relationship, or mulling over entering a relationship with another old flame, you should understand which job this individual will play in your life. All things considered, there's no keeping away from the unavoidable, frequently awkward inquiry we should pose to ourselves: Is this the individual I was limited by predetermination to impart my life to? Or on the other hand did I settle excessively fast into a relationship with somebody who can never finish me?

Regardless of the class you fit into, a few signs obviously frame a perfect partner bond (or an absence of connection) among you and your accomplice. As you go through this rundown, ponder your accomplice or possible accomplice and assess whether they meet the perfect partner standards.

Love is the most impressive power known to mankind. Be that as it may, it can cloud your psyche. Regardless of whether you are frantically enamored, it's not generally clear on the off chance that the individual you're infatuated with is your perfect partner. This is particularly obvious when you need relationship experience, or you've been singed previously.

Your heartfelt perfect partner is quite possibly of the most compelling individual in your life, and there are numerous otherworldly signs that you have a place together. Perfect partner signs are totally obvious once you know them. These signs for the most part include synchronicities, instinct, strong inclination, and other profound signs directly from the Divine.

In spite of the fact that you may likewise have other perfect partners in your companions or family, your heartfelt perfect partner is the individual you are bound to be with for the long stretch. They are the avocado to your toast, with everything-bagel preparing on top. Furthermore, that is the thing makes them so esteemed in your life.

Your heartfelt perfect partner is your otherworldly perfect partner. You two are a heavenly fit, impeccably adjusted in your energy. Your perfect partner is your accomplice in both a companionship and cozy love sense. They are most frequently the individual you wed or go through your time on earth with.

CHAPTER 3

The 10 Elements of a Soulmate

1. It's an inside thing: Depicting how a perfect partner causes you to feel is troublesome. It's a persistent, significant, and waiting feeling that no words can incorporate.

2. Flashbacks: Assuming your accomplice is your perfect partner, odds are the person in question has been available in your previous existences. Perfect partners frequently decide to return together during a similar lifetime and extension each other out in the enormous world. You could out of nowhere and momentarily experience flashbacks of your perfect partner. You could try and feel an odd feeling of history repeating itself, as though the second in time has proactively occurred, maybe quite a while in the past, maybe in an alternate setting.

3. You simply get one another: At any point met two individuals who finish each other's sentences?

Certain individuals assemble that investing an excess of energy, yet I consider it a perfect partner association. You could encounter this with your closest companion or your mom, however it is the indication of a perfect partner when you experience it with your accomplice.

4. You adore for his (or her) defects: No relationship is awesome, and even perfect partner connections will encounter promising and less promising times. In any case, that bond will be a lot harder to break. Perfect partners make some simpler memories tolerating, in any event, figuring out how to adore, each other's defects. Your relationship is bound to be a perfect partner match if you both love each other precisely as you each are, tolerating both the extraordinary and horrendous propensities we as a whole have.

5. Its extreme: A perfect partner relationship might be more extreme than typical connections, in both great and here and there terrible ways. Mainly, in any event, during negative episodes, you're centered around settling the issue and can see past the terrible second.

6. Both of you against the world: Perfect partners frequently see their relationship as "us against the world." They feel so connected together that they're prepared to take on any accomplishment of life, so lengthy they have their perfect partner close by. Perfect partner connections are established on split the difference and solidarity regardless of anything else.

7. You're intellectually indivisible: Perfect partners frequently have a psychological association like twins. They could get the telephone to call each other simultaneously. However life might keep you separated on occasion, your brains will constantly be in order assuming you are perfect partners.

8. You have a solid sense of reassurance and secured: No matter what the orientation of your accomplice, the individual in question ought to continuously cause you to have a good sense of safety and safeguarded. This intends that in the event that you're a man, indeed, your lady ought to cause you to feel safeguarded, as well! Your perfect partner will cause you to feel like you have a divine messenger close by. An individual who plays on your weaknesses, whether deliberately or subliminally, isn't your perfect partner.

9. You can't envision your existence without him (or her):

A perfect partner isn't somebody you can leave that without any problem. It is somebody you can't envision being without, an individual you accept merits staying with and battling for.

10. You look at one another without flinching: Perfect partners will generally investigate each other's eyes while talking more frequently than conventional couples. It works out easily from the firmly established association between them. Looking at an individual without flinching while talking means an elevated degree of solace and certainty.

Whether you're planned by the universe to be perfect partners or two cherishing individuals who have made due with one another's assets and shortcomings, the choice is yours. The excellence of choice is that you can stay in or change any relationship as you see fit. To be with your perfect partner is one of the valuable fortunes of life. Also, assuming that you feel you've seen as your heart's other half, I wish you vast long periods of satisfaction and chuckling, and endless evenings of profound hug, disentangling the secrets of the universe individually.

CHAPTER 4

We ought to talk about all of the signs-sensible, supernatural, and anyway of certifiable wonderful accomplice love.

1. You feel a snapshot of affiliation

Exactly when you at first meet your ideal accomplice, when in doubt, you click instantly. Feeling a second relationship with someone means that you are related eagerly, whether or not you've at any point met. Concerning exuberant affiliations, it spreads the word about no distinction the time span you've someone. In the energy world, the time has pretty much expired. Time is human turn of events.

Spirits are attracted to various spirits. Like attract like. So whether you've known someone for 5 days or 5 minutes, when you feel significant solid areas for that to them, you can trust it's certifiable. You see that soul affiliation feeling immediately. That feeling guides your nature to get to understand that person who could end up being your ideal accomplice. Trust what you feel.

2. You share an outrageous interest

Exactly when you meet your ideal accomplice, you feel a serious interest with them and strong real science. Genuine contemplations appear ok away. There is no doubt they make your heart swell.

You find your ideal accomplice particularly charming, paying little brain to appearance. Whether or not they appear to be a model, the science and interest you feel go far past looks.

Serious genuine interest looks like a fire consuming inside you. It makes it hard to center. You fundamentally ought to go with that person. Additionally, they feel something basically the same as you.

3. You feel like you've known them forever

A clear sign of sincere wonderful accomplice love is a vibe of shared characteristic among you. You both feel like you've known each other forever, whether or not you have not. This sense can be confounding, yet it's very typical among wonderful accomplices.

Perhaps you've encountered them in another life, or on another schedule. Then again, the unmistakable tendency is a branch-off of the soul affirmation you share. Your perfect partner will feel good to be near, and simple to spend time with. You'll appreciate being around them for the lovely solace they bring you. What's more, simultaneously, for the fascination, you feel for them. Solace in addition to extreme actual fascination is a mind blowing blend and a definite sign you've met your perfect partner

4 They are your dearest companion

At the point when you initially meet your perfect partner, there is nobody you'd prefer be near. It won't take long for your old flame to turn into your closest companion when they are without a doubt your perfect partner. Obviously, don't leave your different companions in the residue when this occurs! Simply make a stride back and value that finding both companionship and sentiment in one person is so unique.

Perfect partners are generally companions as a matter of some importance. Yet, when they are sweethearts as well, then they are an accomplice forever. Look no further with regards to sentiment. Also, let nothing interfered with you.

5. You can be your actual self

One more indication of perfect partner love is the capacity to be your actual self with that individual. You can let out your senseless side, get strange, and be wild.

Since you feel totally OK with them, you know you're protected to let down your gatekeeper. You don't need to fear they will pass judgment on you assuming you say or do some unacceptable thing. On the off chance that you accomplish something imbecilic, you can ignore it.

With your perfect partner, you feel sure realizing that they love you for who you are within. You don't need to dazzle them or attempt to make them love you, since they do normally. (Regardless of maybe they haven't said so yet.) And what a positive sentiment that is.

You'll likewise see that envy isn't an issue among you. Since you feel good, esteemed, really focused on, and protected with them, you trust them.

Your perfect partner will show entrust with their activities. As you accomplish for them also, that is the reason neither of you stresses over cheating nor surrender. Neither one individual wants any other person. You two offer an extraordinary obligation of unrestricted love that feels and is secure.

6. There's an unmistakable absence of contention

With your perfect partner in adoration, you will probably see an undeniable absence of contention among you. particularly in the beginning phases of the relationship.

We previously discussed the absence of desire and instability. What's more, the bond you feel.

You will likewise see that you coexist wonderfully with your perfect partner. You seldom contend, battle, or quarrel. Over the long haul you will probably have your highs and lows. Undoubtedly after numerous long stretches of marriage or harmony.

Yet, generally speaking, the show won't be there first and foremost. Or then again regardless of whether by chance it will be, it will determine rapidly. Also, it won't result over the long haul.

There will be times you need to chip away at your relationship and issues emerge, however the general tone of your relationship is serene, cherishing, and secure. Over the long haul and you view at the relationship all in all, joy and harmony dominate any issue. It's very unimaginable.

7. Your gathering occurred in divine timing

Perfect partners who are intended to be together frequently meet with flawless timing when both are single and prepared for a relationship.

In the event that you've at any point met somebody yet the timing was off-base, you can accept it as a sign they weren't intended for you. Since when somebody is intended for you, the timing will be heavenly. At the point when somebody is intended for you, God/the Universe makers the association idiotically simple.

This simple association, the progression of the timing is so correct, is essential for what causes you to feel alright with that individual without skipping a beat. Your chance is in that general area before you and you realize it's intended to be.

Some of the time, another relationship is finishing when you meet your perfect partner. That occurs and is a piece of life. Ideally, everybody in question acts morally. What's intended to be will track down a way.

8. You impart without words

With your perfect partner, you share an elevated association. This implies you can frequently convey without words.

Since you two vibrate at a similar recurrence, you perceive all their non-verbal signs effortlessly. You might try and guess what they might be thinking. Clairvoyance is very normal among perfect partners.

You can tell when they stroll in the entryway on the off chance that they had a decent day or not. You can figure out whether they are in the mind-set to nestle or need some space. You understand what will work on their state of mind.

You're in total agreement with one another's necessities. Furthermore, regard those requirements. You don't get unreliable or irritated at their energies more often than not. You have a good sense of safety, and they treat you consciously, so you don't stress over their temperaments and essentially acknowledge their energy.

This is on the grounds that both of you are thoughtful and wanting to one another that you can judiciously give each other what the other one necessity inwardly. You're both secure in the relationship. Furthermore, sufficiently sympathetic to live as one and act unselfishly.

9. Individuals remark on how superb of a couple you make

Others' thought process ought to frequently be accepted with some hesitancy. Yet, with regards to cherish, focus on the agreement. Does your family like them, as well as the other way around? And your individual companions? Assuming nobody thinks you have a place together, you can ordinarily accept that as a warning (except if every other person is insane, obviously).

With your perfect partner, don't be astonished assuming outsiders comments on how you look great together. Others can frequently get on your association.

I once had a lady in JC Penny tell me (when my better half and I were shopping independently however at that point got together at the register) "Gracious goodness, I saw you around there, and him around there and pondered internally Those individuals seem as though they have a place together. Also, low and observe you are together!"

The vast majority love to see others in affection, and they will get down on it. They will grin and attest your association. In any case, assuming they see issues (particularly your loved ones) they will comment on that, as well. Tune in.

10. You share a comparative lifestyle goals

With your ideal accomplice, you will have a comparable lifestyle targets. Rarely will one individual hankering a house and uber yacht while various necessities an essential life in a humble community.

You are two separate people. Clearly, in any case, you are moreover regularly changed. You share comparative contemplations with respect to what sufficiency, home, family, and love mean. You choose a region to live, also. The Universe commits no blunders in partner wonderful accomplices that need a comparable kind of presence.

Whether or not you have amazingly surprising occupations in contrast with your ideal accomplice, you agree without any problem. It has no effect on the off chance that one individual gets tons more income or has way interesting basic capacities than you, to the extent that your characteristics change.

Wonderful accomplices each need various necessities in the greater sense. Being in all out arrangement about your lifestyle grants both of you to co-make the presence of your dreams.

There are for the most part those situations where one opens the other up to an unanticipated lifestyle. Furthermore, a short time later the other appreciates and recognizes that lifestyle. Keep that Pretty Woman dream, it ends up actually working! yet again regardless, having equivalent lifestyles remains.

11. You participate in similar qualities and morals

This indication of comity is significant and fundamental. For never-ending adoration, you and your perfect partner should participate in similar qualities, ethics, and morals. Those impacts come from the heart. One of you cannot be a sociopath.

You concur genuinely almost about what's good and bad. You share comparable to respectability. Your life has a parent convictions and family values network.

Your interests and feelings will fluctuate a piece on certain issues, however for the greatest possible level of part, are similar to. You treat others with a similar quantum of regard and treat each other with equivalent generosity and respect. Your governmental issues will by and large adjust, or adjust in time.

In any case, additionally perhaps one of you is destined to "open up" the psyche of another If your qualities are feverishly unique. That is plausible. We're in the midst of an "extraordinary arousing" on the planet, all things considered.

Be that as it may, in the long run, and eventually, you should be on a similar sprinter honestly and corruptly. Generally, your hearts should be in a similar spot for your relationship to work long haul. Similar to hearts are a perfect partner sign.

12. Your energy is adjusted agreeably

In a similar sense as the last point, a profound sign you have met your perfect partner is the sensation of concordance you share forcefully.

This implies you're a characteristic match with regards to your character,(and yes contrarics can draw in and balance.) You're additionally a characteristic match as far as how social you like to accompany others,(a daily existence factor) your funny bone, how you manage difficulties, how you oversee diurnal ménage scores, your sex, and the sky is the limit from there.

You'll see that with your perfect partner, you're either authentically undifferentiated from or your disparities cooperate and not against each other.

For outline, one individual might be muddled while one is clean, yet they don't quarrel over drawing. They each give their best for guarantee supportive spots in keeping up with their took part territory. There's equilibrium and concordance in energy, and subsequently harmony in their home.

13. You're normally attracted to them

At the point when you initially meet your perfect partner, you feel normally attracted to them. You may not know why, or without a doubt acknowledge you're so associated with them from the beginning. Particularly on the off chance that you're not searching for affection. Yet, when they show up, you incline toward them directly down. It's not unexpected to see this energy draw sometime later. While you're lounging around at home hitherto and out of nowhere begin permitting that individual. You can't help thinking about why you felt so beguiled. And furthermore you can't quit pondering.

That normal, simple attract to this individual is an otherworldly sign that they're in a huge relationship. That draw is the soul saying Pay consideration!

It's entertaining in light of the fact that sporadically, without a doubt on the off chance that you're passed up gathering somebody, a piece of you isn't shocked. You might have a firm opinion sure that you have a place in one another's lives. Their energy almost feels deplorable, and recognizable as we discussed ahead. You may not put your cutlet on why you feel this strange way. Until you understand they're your perfect partner.

14. You can't quit permitting about them

A definite sign that your perfect partner is showing you, similarly as you're showing them, is the way that they're consistently at the forefront of your thoughts, you basically can't get this individual as far away from you as possible.

It tends to incredibly divert. However, odds are high that they're permitting of you, as well. The energy between you is overwhelming any remaining investigations. For sure after various times together, perfect partners will end up thinking about one another habitually. You might call each other during the day at work, to be sure on the off chance that you just saw each other hours ago over breakfast. You might fantasize about plans with them, intellectually search for them, and the sky is the limit from there. That is the thing you do when you love somebody. Notwithstanding, they wouldn't be on your see any problems so much, If you couldn't have cared less. Perfect partners are permitting each other as often as possible.

15. You're each the a la mode translation of yourselves together

Perfect partners draw out the polished in one another. Certainly, we as a whole have our minutes, however generally you're your smart translation of yourself together. You're a superior individual with that exceptional individual than without. You're happier and calmer. You’re staying out of trouble and keeping yourself in line. It’s intriguing how people who have been together for a while frequently come to the point where they consider parting ways. They may ask to date other people, that kind of thing. Questioning everything is vital in life. But with your soulmate, you'll fluently re-confirm that you want them and only them. You know that your soulmate is your stylish match. You don’t give up on them, and they don’t give up on you. You’re married

CHAPTER 5

Is your long-lasting crush now your beau/sweetheart? That is amazing! Presently, changing your relationship status is only the start of what will be an exciting ride. One of the difficulties of being seeing someone how to safeguard it and make it last, and it takes something beyond your "I love you" to get that going.

All in all, how might you safeguard your relationship and make it last? These tips are exceptionally made for you:

1. Remain open to one another.

You might have heard this multiple times, yet open correspondence is the groundwork of a sound relationship. You got issues with how your accomplice is treating you? Let him/her have some familiarity with it. Do you respect somebody in the workplace? In any case, educate your accomplice. Assuming that you make it your propensity to be available to one another, you can deal with any potential issues directly.

2. Remain genuine.

In accordance with being available to one another is tell the truth to your accomplice. Be straightforward regardless of whether means harming him/her. On the off chance that you're not content with how the ongoing relationship is going, be straightforward still. In the event that you've committed a mix-up, be sufficiently dependable to enlighten your accomplice. It would be quite hard, yet by the day's end, your accomplice would in any case value your genuineness.

3. Trust one another.

Do you generally open or even hack your accomplice's web-based entertainment account since you're concerned he/she is conversing with another person? That is one appearance that you have zero faith in your accomplice. Therefore, you will have unending trivial battles, which will before long reason more pressing issues. In spite of the fact that trust issues have their own story, it is an unquestionable necessity to trust your accomplice. Recall that a relationship based on trust is a sort of relationship that endures.

4. Remain faithful and dedicated.

For you to become somebody who should be relied upon, you must be unwavering. Be unwavering in light of the fact that he/she is all that anyone could need. Be unwavering in light of the fact that there's just a single him/her on the planet. Be reliable on the grounds that it's the correct thing to do. Be devoted on the grounds that you can't stand to hurt or lose him/her.

5. Remain open to changes.

Change is unavoidable while you develop as a person. Your accomplice may not be a similar individual you met when the relationship began, and you want to acknowledge that. Indeed, even you will change. Recollect that both of you actually have a great deal to encounter and investigate throughout everyday life. Try not to be that somebody that could impede his/her development. Rather, show up for one another when those changes occur.

6. Remain cozy with one another.

Actual touch is an unquestionable requirement in each relationship. It's one method for keeping the fire consuming. It's one method for communicating your friendship to one another, so invest some energy finding each other more. Invest an energy to see the value in one another more. Be much more insane about one another. Keep some degree of closeness since it's tomfoolery and provocative, and that is the manner by which your relationship ought to be.

7. Continue to attempt new things.

The relationship will in general get exhausting assuming that you feel like you know one another so well as of now. Each relationship goes through that stage, yet it might be a stage assuming you follow through with something. Rather than following a similar daily schedule, how about you attempt new things?

Accomplish something insane together. Be unconstrained together. Giggle and get lost together; that is one of the marvels of being seeing someone.

8. Shock one another.

Beside attempting new things, ensure that you actually get to amaze your accomplice occasionally. Causc your accomplice to feel like you're actually standing by to at last get his/her yes. Make him/her vibe unique in your own basic and imaginative ways. It certainly is one of the ways of making him/her long for you considerably more.

9. Remain delightful.

Try not to simply remain delightful for your accomplice; remain wonderful for yourself. Remain sure. Lighthearted about yourself. Be agreeable in your skin. Be enabled, and your excellence will emanate from the inside. Easily, your accomplice will be overwhelmed with passion for you.

10. Permit each other to be free.

Your accomplice may be giving you that option to define a few limits, however don't make him/her vibe smothered. Indeed, it's sweet to call him/her yours, yet recollect that you don't claim the individual. Regard his/her opportunity. Permit your accomplice to continue to find himself/herself. Permit each other to in any case do your desired things while remaining committed in the relationship.

11. Support one another.

About giving your accomplice the opportunity that he/she really wants, you should be his/her emotionally supportive network. Support your accomplice in his/her objectives. Try not to miss the main dates. Show up for him/her since you need to observe each achievement in his//her life. All the more significantly, you need to show up for him/her in his/her haziest times.

12. Remember your own existence.

Investing quality energy with your accomplice is an unquestionable necessity to make the relationship develop, yet investing some time for yourself is likewise an absolute requirement to make yourself develop. Partake in your alone time. Keep each other's independence. Doing this every so often will lead you to miss one another and feel invigorated when you return to one another's arms.

13. Find opportunity to pay attention to one another.

At times, individuals misjudge the force of tuning in. Truly, keeping the groundwork of the relationship solid is one mystery. Tune in before you lash out. Tune in before you toss out those terrible words. Tune in before you become silly. Listen on the grounds that you're the absolute first individual he/she would believe you should pay attention to him/her.

14. Regard one another.

In particular, regard your accomplice; that is a brilliant rule. Regard his/her choices. Regard his/her standards throughout everyday life. Regard his/her loved ones. Regard him/her as your accomplice. Regard him/her personally.

Without a doubt, focusing on a relationship isn't simply a question of enjoying or cherishing one another. You're one fortunate individual to have found the individual you can call your accomplice, so you should give your very best for show to what lengths you will go for him/her to be a piece of and remain in your life.

www.ingramcontent.com/pod-product-compliance
Lightning Source LLC
LaVergne TN
LVHW052105160826
845678LV00015B/3371

* 9 7 9 8 8 4 6 5 6 2 3 6 3 *